How To Use This Book

If you're reading this book, it means that you need a little help talking to teachers.

I've been on the teacher side of many parent-teacher meetings. I've also coached many parents as they prepared for teacher meetings. One things I've noticed: the more prepared the parent is for the meeting, the more productive the meeting becomes.

This book will help you get prepared. You want to get your message across in a way that is calm, clear, concise, and respectful. You want to work with your child's teacher to ensure the best possible outcomes for the school year.

Remember that while you have one child in the classroom, the teacher has twenty, or twenty-five, or thirty children. Each of these children has different needs. As a parent, you have a limited amount of time to establish a good relationship, get information, make a request, or follow up on a plan. Your communications with your child's teacher need to be effective.

This is where the book comes in.

I provide sample scripts based on real conversations, emails, and meetings that I have had over the years. These are meetings where the parents walked away happy, the child got what she/he needed, and I felt like we were all on the same team. Everyone won.

This book contains sample scripts, email messages, and conversation starters to help you communicate effectively in any school situation. Keep in mind that these are *samples*: starting points for effective communications. Please be sure to modify them to reflect your child.

These are scripts that I have found to be most effective. However, your experience might be different or an alternative message might work better for you. Different teachers also react to messages and communication styles differently, so tailor your communication to your teacher as well.

Finally, the communication is only as good as the messenger. No matter what situation you find yourself in, it is vitally important to remain calm and respectful. Try to speak and write with kindness, or at least politeness.

If you have questions or need resources tailored to your specific situation, I am happy to consult with you. Contact me at milkidsed@gmail.com.

Learn more at: MilKidsEd.com

Best wishes for improved teacher communications!

Meg Flanagan, M. Ed.

Before Your Meeting

Do your homework

Before going to a meeting, make sure you know what you are talking about. This is especially true for meetings that you have requested or that could be contentious.

You definitely don't want to walk blind into a meeting about your child's negative behavior!

Communication

Keep the lines of communication open with the teacher or administration before the meeting.

Confirm the time, date, and location of your meeting several days prior.

Keep communication logs. Record phone calls and save emails or notes. Bring relevant documents to the meeting

What to bring

To have a successful meeting, it helps to be prepared. You should bring a few key items with you:

- pencil or pen, plus back ups

- notebook or paper

- supporting documents

    - school work

    - tests

    - assessment results

    - damaged items (see: Negative conference, called by parents: behavior/bullying)

    - documentation of concerns, communication, etc.

Be realistic

This is perhaps the most important point. Every single child is different. They all learn in different ways, have unique talents, and abilities.

Your child is unique, too. While we all want our children to succeed beyond our wildest dreams, not every child will progress through school or life in the same way.

Before your meeting, sit down and really think about your child. Consider:

- What level is your child currently functioning at academically?

- What are his/her behavior challenges?

- Are there any diagnoses of disabilities or health impairments that might impact education?

- What is the purpose of this meeting? Remember that you might not be able to cover everything in one meeting, so pick out the most important talking points.

- Given my child's current academic functioning and behavior concerns (if any), what is realistic?

This deep questioning is very important, but can be hard for parents to accomplish independently. This is where an education consultant is a valuable resource. As an objective third party, an education consultant can review academic records, test results, and observe your child at school. With this information, they have a good snapshot of where your child is presently functioning and what the future might hold.

If you think that your family might need help objectively assessing your child, hire an educational consultant to help you work through the process. By adding this person to your team you can also reap major benefits during meetings and in school communication.

Introduce Your Child
Meet the Teacher Day, PK-5/6

Meet the Teacher Day script

Teacher: Hello, welcome to our classroom

Parent: Hello, I'm (Your Name) and this is my son/daughter, (insert Child's Name here).

Teacher: Hello, (Child's Name)

At this point, the teacher should direct you/your child to his/her desk and give basic directions about the classroom and/or school.

Take this opportunity to look around the room, locate your child's desk and navigate from the classroom to the bathroom, cafeteria and specialist classrooms (art, language, physical education, music, etc.).

This is also the time to give the teacher your copy of <u>Meet the Teacher</u>. You should also fill out any contact forms the teacher provides.

It's okay to take the lead when meeting a new teacher for children from pre-kindergarten (PK) through middle to late elementary school. After this, Meet the Teacher Day seems to fade away. If your child's middle or high school has a similar day, your child should be taking the lead and asking at least some of these questions.

Basic questions to ask

- Where is the (location of another room in the school)? This could be the bathroom, art room, cafeteria, nurse's office, etc.

- What time is lunch/recess?

- What is your homework policy?

- What is the best way to contact you?

- What is your policy on meetings? Phone calls?

- Does your classroom have a website and/or newsletter?

- How can I help you? Do you need volunteers or supplies?

- Do you have a policy on food or drink, other than water?

For children with Special Education needs

Use this sample script to share information about your child's Special Education needs, an upcoming deployment or other situation that might affect the classroom and learning situation.

Teacher: Hi, I'm (Teacher's Name). What's your name?

Parent: I'm (Your Name) and this is (Child's Name). When you get a minute, could I talk to you quickly about some things you should be aware of for this year?

Teacher: Of course!

Parent (during that quiet moment): I just wanted to share that (Child's Name) needs some extra attention due to (insert reason here).

At this point, spell out what your child needs:

- seating close to the teacher

- extra time on assignments

- access to the school counselor

- recommendations to a tutor

- fidget items

- extra reminders

- constant contact with you

- food or environmental allergies and precautions

- medications taken daily during school hours

- anything else the teacher needs to know on Day 1

Start a brief discussion now, and then request a meeting during the first few weeks of school. This conversation is simply to put your child's need on the teacher's radar, not to cover them in depth.

Meeting the Teacher, 6-12

First, back off. Your child is becoming a young adult. From here on out, most of his/her interactions with teachers will be handled on his/her own. And that's just fine.

Practice this script with your child

Teacher: Hi, I'm Teacher's Name. I'll be your (insert subject here) teacher.

Student: Hi, I'm (Child's Name). I'm really excited to be in your class this year. Can you tell me about your:

- homework policy

- grading policy

- late work policy

- teaching style (lecture, group projects, interactive, small groups, etc.)

Student: I also need to let you know that I might need help with:

- keeping track of assignments

- sitting close to the board

- taking notes

- extra time on tests

- I have an IEP or 504 Plan

- controlling life-threatening allergies

- taking medication daily

Student/Parent: I know you probably don't have time right now to talk about this in detail, but could we set up a meeting in the next few weeks? I'd like to figure out how I can do my best in this class.

Teacher: Great! Thanks for letting me know about this. I would be happy to sit down with you as soon as possible. Let's talk next week.

Conferences and Meetings
Positive Meeting, No Questions

No matter what grade your child is in currently, you will likely have at least one scheduled parent-teacher conference near the beginning of the school year. These generally occur after the first set of report card or progress reports have been sent home. Scheduled parent-teacher conferences like these are usually just to discuss the report card, your child's grades, and the teacher's expectations or observations. This is a great time to ask question, although you certainly do not have to if you are satisfied with what your child is accomplishing or the teacher's explanation of his/her class.

These meetings are also very brief, usually 15-25 minutes long. There are many other parents with meetings scheduled before or after your own meeting. This is not a reason to shorten your meeting, but do try to be gracious if another parent's meeting runs a little long.

Teacher: Hello! I'm thrilled that (Child's Name) is doing really well in school. His/her report card is showing real progress.

At this point, the teacher might pull out work samples to illustrate your child's progress, explain about the class , review grading and homework policy, or ask questions about your child's life at home.

If you do not have any further questions, you can conclude this meeting quickly.

Teacher: Do you have any questions?

Parent(s): No, I am very pleased with his/her progress.

Teacher: Great! Let me know how I can help you or if you have any questions in the future.

If you are satisfied, your meeting can be over. Remember that you can ask for another meeting at any point during the school year to check on your child's progress or ask questions.

Positive Meeting, Questions

Of course, every parent has questions about their child and school. So after your teacher tells you how amazing your child is, ask these questions:

- What are my child's weaknesses? How do you know?

- How can I help my child improve in these areas?

- What are my child's strengths? How do you know?

- How can I continue to challenge my student in these areas?

- What is my child like in the classroom? Is s/he disruptive?

- How can we work together to correct these issues (if any)?

- What are my child's friends like?

- Are there any social issues that I need to be aware of?

- What special opportunities at school might benefit my child? How can we sign up for these?

- Are there tutors available through the school? Do any teachers provide tutoring? Can you help me connect with them?

- How are you using computers and technology in the classroom? Roughly how much time is spent on computers or on other technology during the school day?

- Are there any projects coming up that I need to know about?

- How can I help you in the classroom?

- What tests are coming up?

- Are these tests based on what you've been teaching in class? Or are they benchmarking tests?

- How will these tests be used in the classroom?

- Will the results affect my child? How?

Whatever you ask, be prepared for honest answers. Keep asking questions until you are completely clear. If you have additional concerns, now is the time to address them.

Neutral Meeting, Special Education Information

This is the meeting you asked for during Meet the Teacher. Your goal is to discuss your child's IEP or 504 Plan, goals, accommodations and ways that your child learns best. Before the meeting, make copies of your child's IEP, 504 Plan. Having this data on hand will help you to reference specifics. Leave a copy with the teacher when your meeting ends and keep a copy for yourself as well.

Parent: Thanks for meeting with me. I want to touch base on (Child's Name)'s IEP/504 Plan. I'm sure that you have it on file, but I brought a copy for each of us just in case.

Teacher: Thanks! I do have a copy, but I can make notes on this one.

Parent: I'd like to start off by talking about (pick one):

- seating

- proximity to the teacher

- proximity to the whiteboard/smartboard

- extended time on assignments

- modified work

- testing accommodations

- classroom set-up

- behavior monitoring/behavior plan

- work monitoring

- assistive technology

- transportation

- things teachers have done in the past

- parent/teacher communication

- life threatening allergies or other medical concerns

Explain the concern you have, how it is related to the IEP/504 Plan and how this has been handled in the past. Explain what you have observed to work and not work for your child.

Ask how the current teacher would be able to address these concerns.

Repeat for each area of concern you have or each thing that the teacher needs to be aware of. This is where the checklist you made before the meeting will be useful.

Make notes on your copy of the IEP of how the teacher will be helping your child, what will be happening and how often it will be happening. Ask who else will be involved in teaching your child (paraprofessional, specialists, Special Education teacher, etc.). Ask that the teacher communicate the main points of the conversation to these people.

Parent: Thank you so much for meeting with me today. I so appreciate that you took time out of your busy schedule for this. Please let me know how I can help you this school year and support your classroom techniques at home.

Teacher: Thank you for sharing this information with me. It will definitely help me in teaching your son/daughter this year.

Before you leave, request a meeting between now and Parent-Teacher conferences at the end of the term or quarter.

The next meeting will be a check-in to determine how your child is doing in the classroom. Follow the script for Positive Meeting, Questions on page 9.

Negative Conference, Called by the Teacher

Sometimes your child's teacher will need to speak with you, immediately and directly, as a result of negative actions your child has taken.

This could be:

- disruptive behavior

- inappropriate language or behavior

- academic concerns

- violence

- bullying

If you are about to have a potentially negative meeting, know that the teacher is not your enemy. S/he is on your side.

It is hard to remember this, especially when emotions are running high. By preparing for your meeting and following a script, it can help to remove some of the emotions and use logic to address the concerns.

During the meeting, follow this order of business:

- **Listen:** listen to everything the teacher has to say about the situation

- **Ask:** ask questions specifically about the situation, such as:

  - *How do you know that (the situation) happened?*

  - *Have you taken any action in school yet to correct (this situation)?*

  - *What were the steps followed prior to contacting me about (this situation)?*

  - *Where do we go from here?*

Use the <u>worksheets</u> at the back of this book to help you prepare for a successful meeting.

Listen: as the teacher responds to your questions, listen carefully. If you feel that something is wrong or incorrect, make a note of it. Wait until the teacher is finished to offer your own thoughts.

- **Collaborate:** work with the teacher to find a solution to the situation. Write down what the solution is and the steps in that process. Make sure you both have a copy and set a meeting in 1-2 weeks to check in.

Academic conference script

Adapt this script as needed and as the situation demands. Remember that staying on script can help to keep the meeting positive and productive. To solve the problem and help your child, everyone will need to work together.

Teacher: As you know, we are here to talk about (Child's Name)'s grades recently. They are not where they should be. *Teacher should provide a review of child's grades, like a progress report or report card.*

Parent: Could you please explain your grading process?

Teacher: *explains grading process, usually a rating scale, 0-100 percentage, a cumulative system, or some combination of these.*

Parent: Could you please walk me through the assignments that caused him/her the most trouble? I'd like to know what the expectations were, see the directions and grading standards, and look at my child's finished product.

Teacher: *shows parent the requested information*

Parent: Where do you think the issue happened? Why do you think it happened? *Repeat for each work sample shown*

Teacher: *depending on the work sample, answers could include: studying, attending to directions/details, following written directions, lack of focus, inattention during work time, lack of effort, more serious academic concerns (Special Education)*

Parent: I know you are an excellent teacher, and are probably already addressing many of these issues in the classroom. Can you tell me what you have tried so far? What seems to be working or not working?

Teacher: *explains interventions. These could include: extra time, open notebook/textbook during tests, visual aides, written aides, visual schedules, checklists, priority seating, one-on-one review, small group lessons, individual lessons, extra review time, decreased work, modified expectations, modified work, scaled scores, Special Education consult, behavioral consult, referral to the school counselor, etc.*

Parent: What are the next steps at school if his/her grades do not improve, even with all of the extra things that you are doing?

Teacher: *explains next steps: Response to Intervention (RtI), Special Education referral, failing the class, repeating the grade, failing to graduate*

Parent: What can I do at home to help you?

Teacher: *explains what to do at home: tutoring, medical evaluation, academic support websites, parental request for Special Education testing, reward system for good grades, etc.*

Parent: Just to review, my son/daughter has poor grades in (subject or subjects). You have seen this mostly in (name type of work OR in all areas). In school, you have tried (list teacher interventions). Even with these in place, my child is still not working to his/her potential. Your next steps in school are (list possible interventions). At home, I can help by (list things you are willing or able to do at home). Does that seem accurate?

Teacher: Yes, that about sums it up.

Parent: Can we write up a plan of action that we can both work on? I'd really like to see what's going to happen next listed out so that we can all stay on track with this.

Teacher: That sounds great.

Parent: Can we plan to meet in a few weeks? I want to make sure that the things we have talked about today are happening, and working. If things aren't improving, I would like to be able to change course sooner rather than later.

Teacher: *suggests dates and times for meetings or suggests that s/he needs to check the calendar for the best dates.*

Parent: I will email you this week to let you know what works for me.

Behavior conference script

This is a basic script and can be adapted for use in a variety of situations. If you need help in creating a more customized script, contact me to learn about consulting services.

Behavior conferences can be especially challenging. Sometimes parents can feel like comments about their child's behavior are a reflection on their parenting skills. This is not the case.

Most behavior conferences are called for the same reason as academic conferences: a child is not meeting expectations, it has become serious or detrimental to his/her education or safety, and a plan needs to be created to correct his/her current path.

At a behavior meeting it is important that you prepare yourself to hear unflattering things about your child. It is vital that you come with your checklist of questions. By following this script, you will be able to stay on track and remain logical instead of emotional. Remember that everyone is here because they care about your child and they are concerned about the current situation.

Teacher: Thank you for coming in to meet with me. As you know, there are some concerns with (Child's Name)'s behavior. S/he has (*Teacher explains your child's behavior*).

Parent: Thank you for letting us know about this issue. We definitely want to resolve this issue quickly. Can you please tell me:

- when you first noticed this type of behavior?

- where this behavior has been happening most often?

- if there is a specific time of day you are seeing this behavior more often than other times?

- if there is a person or group being affected by this behavior (*for physical/verbal aggression, bullying, inappropriate language, etc.*)?

- have you observed this behavior personally? If not, who has informed you of the behavior?

- what you have already done to find a solution in school?

Ask each question one at a time and take notes as the teacher responds. Pay particular attention to the interventions that have already been attempted.

Parent: Why do you think that these interventions have not been successful? What are our next steps?

*Keep in mind: the teacher gains nothing from setting your child up or falsely reporting a negative behavior. If you are having a meeting like this, it is likely that the teacher has been observing this behavior for quite some time. If you do have concerns, please use the **script on page 17** for contesting the validity of the school's concerns.*

Teacher: Explains interventions again, noting why they might have failed to change the behavior. Explains next steps:

- detention

- suspension (requires a meeting with administration)

- loss of privileges (recess, free time, fun time, class parties)

- natural consequences (clean up mess s/he created, apologize in writing or in person to injured parties, monetary payments for damaged property, etc.)

- counseling with on-staff student counselor or social worker

Parent: What can we do at home to support you?

Teacher: *Examples could include loss of at-home privileges (screen time, parties, play time, sports, etc.), extra chores, etc.*

Parent: I'd like to check back in with you in a few weeks to see where we are with this issue. I definitely do not want this to continue to be a problem in your classroom.

Set a date/time for your next meeting. Repeat and adapt this script until the problem is resolved.

Behavior conference, contested

If you believe that your child is not exhibiting the behavior(s) in question, it is your right as a parent to contest this at the meeting. Keep in mind that teachers take these issues very seriously, and rarely make random accusations. Often data has been collected and observations made over an extended period of time, depending on the seriousness and duration of the issue. Teachers also have nothing to gain from this type of meeting, whereas a child has everything to lose from behaving poorly in school.

You might also feel that a consequence is too harsh or doesn't "fit the crime," so to speak. This meeting is the time to bring that up.

After hearing about the issue and asking the first set of questions from the behavior conference script on page 15, delve a little deeper.

Parent: I appreciate what you are saying, but I'm having a hard time believing that my child could have done this or behaved this way. Do you have further evidence that what you are describing has happened? Are there behavior logs or reports? Do you have a record of the consequences my child has already received?

Teacher: *produces additional evidence, if any.*

Parent: *review evidence, asking for explanations as needed. Based on what you are seeing in this evidence, decide if you want to continue to dispute the issue.*

Parent: *select your response(s):*

- I'm just not seeing a clear pattern of behavior in these records. Unless you failed to write down every instance, this seems to be a random occurrence. I don't consider this to be serious at this time. Please continue to keep me in the loop if this continues.

- While I appreciate your concern, I don't think that this behavior is out of control or impacting his/her education at this time. Would you consider tracking it for a longer period of time so we can have more evidence for a later meeting?

- Even with this evidence, I'm simply not able to believe that my child is capable of this behavior. I will be speaking with him/her tonight about it. I will be mentioning this meeting and what you have told me. Can we reconvene later this week or next week to continue this conversation? I'd like my child to be present at our next meeting. I would also like to have the principal or vice principal present.

- Thank you for sharing this with me. I would like to think about what you have shared. Could we schedule another meeting, with my child and the principal or vice principal, for later this week or next week?

- I understand that my child has done something wrong, but I don't think that these consequences are equivalent to the actions. Can we discuss alternatives?

- I believe that this behavior might be as a result of (a situation at home/out of school). I'd really like to involve the school counselor or social worker. Can we work together to develop a plan to help curb these behaviors?

- I believe that these behaviors might be a symptom of (medical or mental health condition). I'd like to refer my child for Special Education assessment. I'll be formally requesting it tomorrow, and contacting my child's doctor right after this meeting to schedule an appointment. Until we hear back one way or the other, can we create a behavior plan to help this situation?

- I believe these behaviors are as a result of (in-school social situation). I'd like to learn more about this before we proceed with consequences for my child.

- I believe that this behavior is as a result of (boredom, lack of challenge, too much work, too little work, too difficult, etc.). I'd like to talk about (increasing workload, opportunities for extension in the classroom, modifying work, scaling back work) to see if a change in this area helps. Can we work out a plan for that? Then we can meet again in a few weeks to discuss progress or lack of progress.

Teacher: *The teacher might either agree or disagree with your request.*

If the teacher agrees with your request, please keep an open mind and be ready for the next meeting. If the behavior continues, be ready to work with the teaching team on consequences and behavior plans.

If the behavior is serious, has affected other children/adults negatively, or is potentially violent, expect the teacher to disagree with your request. This situation will likely be immediately referred to the principal or vice principal. Be prepared to continue this discussion.

Negative Conference, Called by Parents
Academic conference, low grades/lack of progress

Use this script when your child is not succeeding in school and has low grades. Remember that staying on script and following your talking points checklist can help the meeting to remain positive and productive.

Parent: Thanks for meeting with me. I know you have limited time and lots to do, so I'll cut to the chase. My child's grades are much lower than I expected. Can you tell me what is going on?

Teacher: Sure! I've also been concerned about his/her grades. This is what I've been seeing in school. *The teacher will let you know about your child's behavior, work ethic, and study habits in school. Be prepared to hear about:*

- lack of focus

- talkativeness, excessive socialization

- lack of interest in work

- trouble following directions

- trouble organizing materials

- lack of effort

- not asking for help

- not accepting offers of help

- forgetfulness

- missing or late work

- trouble using available support materials (open book tests, calculators, agenda books, etc.)

- behavior issues impacting academic success

Take notes on what the teacher is saying about your child's in-school effort, behavior, and focus.

Parent: Thanks for shedding some light on what is happening in the classroom. What have you been doing so far to help my child with these issues?

Teacher: *details interventions. Expect to hear about:*

- small group lessons

- one-on-one lessons

- review work

- extended time on assignments

- modified length or content of assignments

- teacher assistance on work

- seating arrangement

- behavior plans

- rewards/consequences systems

- peer models/supports

- work plans

- Response to Intervention (RtI)

Parent: Thank you for helping my child. Do any of these things seem to work? When will we be seeing the progress from your efforts?

Teacher: *explains what is working/not working and how long it will take to see results.*

Parent: Ok, what can I do at home to support you in school?

Teacher: *tutoring, reviewing work with child, reviewing homework, practicing skills online using school approved websites, reading, writing, cooking, etc.*

Parent: Should I be concerned about Special Education at this point? If not right now, at what point does that become a concern? What do I do if it comes to that?

Teacher: *explains the Special Education process and any concerns s/he has right now.*

Parent: What if these interventions and programs don't work? What will be the next step?

Teacher: *explains next steps.*

Parent: Is there a danger of repeating this grade/course as a result of his/her current grades?

Teacher: *explains risks.*

Parent: (*if behavior is a concern*) Why do you think s/he is behaving that way? Do you notice it happening at any particular time, in a particular subject, or in a particular location?

Teacher: *offers observations.*

Parent: What strategies are in place to help with the behavior? If s/he is able to control that behavior, do you think his/her grades will improve?

Teacher: *offers opinion on chances for better grades, explains behavior interventions.*

Parent: If the behavior doesn't improve, what would be the next steps?

Teacher: *explains the next steps.*

Parent: think I understand what you will be doing for my child in terms of behavior and academics (*sum up what you ahem talked about, use your notes to help you*). I think I'll have to make a plan to support this at home. Can we check back in with each other in four to six weeks? I'd like to keep this situation from getting out of control.

Agree on a meeting time and date. Keep a copy of your notes from this meeting handy for reference.

Academic conference, lack of enrichment or extension

Use this script when your child is gifted and talented or very intelligent, and you feel that s/he is not being challenged enough in school.

Keep in mind that you are likely asking the teacher to describe programs that are already in place in the classroom, but which your child may or may not be accessing.

You may also be asking an already overworked professional to put in even more (unpaid) hours to design lessons specifically for your child. Be kind, be gracious, and plan to be proactive at home.

Parent: Thank you for meeting with me today. I'd like to talk about how we can work together to help (Child's Name) really meet his/her potential.

Teacher: Great! I'm looking for the same thing!

Parent: Can you tell me what you are already doing to help extend and enrich the lessons?

Teacher: I am doing/I already have in place: *(may list one or more of the following)*

- fast finisher work: extra lesson-connected work and project for students who finish work quickly and completely

- small groups: leveled groups of students who are working on slightly different projects connected to the same core content

- reading groups: students are grouped by reading level and/or interest; read just-right level books and discuss their reading with the teacher; complete projects and assignments connected to the reading at a variety of levels

- group projects: students work in leveled or mixed groups of students on hands-on projects connected to the lessons

- free choice projects: students are encouraged to explore topics that interest them in teacher-guided independent projects

- gifted and talented programs: students are pulled from the regular classroom to work with a teacher certified in teaching gifted/talented children; students work on grade-level connected materials that encourages problem solving, outside of the box thinking, and exploration of content; student must qualify through assessments and/or teacher referrals for this program

- challenge materials: similar to fast finisher; student choose academically challenging material to work on at their own pace after all assigned work is completed

Parent: Can you tell me about which of these options my child is using?

Teacher: *explains how student is using built-in enrichment opportunities.*

Parent: Do you track students who are doing these extensions? What happens to the work they complete?

Teacher: *explains tracking method, extension work collection and assessment methods*

Parent: Do you think that my child is being challenged enough? Why or why not?

Teacher: *explains thoughts on this question.*

Parent: Do you encourage students to use the built -n extension options? How so?

Teacher: *explains methods for pushing students to their highest potential. Keep in mind that many intelligent students also enjoy reading quietly, drawing, or reviewing taught materials after assignments are complete.*

Parent: I would like my child to be required/encouraged to complete enrichment work after assignments are complete. How can we make this happen?

Teacher: *suggests motivation techniques, tracking charts, additional assignments, private work contracts, etc.*

Parent: Excellent! I'd like to check back in with you in a month or so to see where my child is at with the extension work and if s/he is continuing to be challenged and extended beyond the typical lessons. What can we do at home to help (Child's Name)?

Teacher: *Offers suggestions for activities, programs, and websites that might provide additional activities to help your child at home.*

Set up a future meeting before you end the meeting.

As appropriate: ask about the Gifted and Talented (GT) program

Parent: *(if child isn't in GT)* Is my child eligible, in your mind, for the gifted and talented program?

Teacher: *explains eligibility rules and where this child is on the GT spectrum.*

Parent: What can I do, or can we do together, to help enroll my child in the GT program?

Teacher: *explains what, if anything, can be done to help your child's chances of being accepted into the GT program.*

Parent: *(if child is in GT)* Can you tell me what the gifted and talented schedule is? When is my child being pulled? What is s/he missing in the classroom? Is s/he held accountable for that work? What is s/he doing in the GT room?

Teacher: *answers questions, will likely refer you to the GT teacher for specifics on the GT program.*

Parent: Is my child benefitting from the GT program at this time? Why or why not?

Teacher: *likely refers you to the GT teacher; repeat this question to that teacher; take notes.*

Before you end the meeting and leave the school, pop into the GT teacher's room and schedule a meeting with him/her. If the teacher isn't there, send an email before you leave the building requesting a meeting.

If possible, try to coordinate any follow-up meetings to include both the general education teacher(s) and the GT teacher.

Behavior conference, bullying/other behavior concerns

Childhood is full of tough situations. Some of these situations are harder than others, like bullying. If you feel that your child is being targeted at school, contact the teacher immediately via phone or email to arrange an in-person meeting.

Bullying: classified by repeated instances of verbal and/or physical abuse or violence, intimidation, coercion, extortion, teasing, shaming, or social exclusion

Parent: Thank you for meeting with me. I'd like to talk about:

- bullying on the playground

- bullying on the bus

- bullying in the classroom

- bullying in the bathrooms

- bullying in the hallways/passing between classes

- verbal abuse by another student (name calling, teasing, etc.)

- verbal abuse by another staff member in the classroom (not the teacher, include administration in this meeting)

- physical abuse by another student (hitting, grabbing, kicking, etc.)

- physical abuse by another staff member (not the teacher, include administration in this meeting)

- social exclusion or shaming by "friends"

- extortion (lunch money, pocket change, schoolwork, etc.)

- coercion (forcing child to perform bullying behavior to another child out of fear of reprisals)

- intimidation by another student

- intimidation by a staff member (not the teacher, include administration in this meeting)

Describe the situation as you know it, give dates/times, specific actions, reaction of your child, and how it is affecting him/her. Explain what you understand to have happened at school as a consequence of these behaviors. Ask the teacher to elaborate.

Teacher: Thank you so much for coming to me with these concerns. Obviously, I take this very seriously and want to resolve it as soon as possible. Let me tell you what I have seen at school.

Teacher explains what s/he has seen or what has been reported to him/her. S/he explains steps s/he has taken to prevent further instances of these situations or consequences that have been given out. Teacher should explain your child's role (aggressor, victim, or both) in the situation, as s/he sees it.

Teacher: I hope that my observations of what is going on have shed some light on the situation.

Parent: *(if you are satisfied or agree with the teacher's assessment of the situation)*Yes, it has. Where do we go from here? I definitely want to resolve this situation or remove my child from this situation as soon as possible.

Teacher: Here are some solutions that I can start right now:

- change seats

- change lockers or similar school storage place

- alert recess/bus monitors to situation

- alert principal/vice principal to the situation (if not already done)

- provide alternate recess options (indoor recess with teacher, joining a physical education or art class held at the same time {with permission from those teachers}, counseling session during recess)

- assign seats at lunch

- conference with aggressors or all students involved in the situation

- counseling services during the school day

- counseling/mediation services with others involved in the situation

- teacher monitoring of situation during recess

- start subtle praise program: complimenting child on positive character traits to boost self-esteem and confidence; help to negate the bullying or social isolation s/he is experiencing; done subtly so as not to draw additional attention to your child

- monitor the situation, take notes and communicate with you about the situation

- teacher meeting with parents of other students (you would not be asked to these meetings due to confidentiality)

- teacher meeting with parents of all students involved (only with agreement from all parents)

- teacher discusses consequences with admin/parents of other students involved; consequence system started and monitored

Teacher: Which (of these) do you think will be most effective for your child? I don't want to make him/her an even bigger target through very overt action or embarrass him/her in school.

Parent: I think that (options) would be best. How will you be following up on this situation?

Teacher: *explains monitoring/reporting system*

Parent: If this doesn't end, what are the next steps?

Teacher: The next things that might happen are:

- involvement of principal/vice principal

- further mediation or counseling, either alone or with the other students

- classroom change

- severe consequences for aggressors (detention, suspension, expulsion as determined by school's code of conduct and disciplinary guidelines)

- change of transportation for your child or other children involved (bus suspension, parent transport to school, etc.)

Some of these options, like change of transportation, would require you to change your schedule or work with the school. Be prepared to step up to the situation for your child.

Parent: These sound like good options. Let's plan on trying (options) beginning tomorrow or as soon as possible. Can we try these for a few weeks, and then check back in for an update?

Teacher: Perfect. Let's schedule that meeting. In the meantime, I'll keep my administration and counseling staff in the loop and provide you with updates as needed via email or phone. Does that sound ok?

Parent: That sounds very reasonable. Thank you so much for being so supportive.

Schedule your next meeting and keep the notes from this meeting. Check in via a casual email at least once weekly between in-person meetings.

Note: You do not have to involve counseling staff or services at the school. That is your choice and your right. You may decline. Even if they don't personally see your child, they will likely know about the situation in basic terms. Teachers often seek the advice of social workers and school counselors to problem solve or seek additional resources.

However, administration will likely be involved in much of the decision making for this situation and may even have final say over consequences or plans of action.

Special Education, non-compliance with IEP

This kind of meeting could be more of a fact-finding mission. You will likely be trying to determine if your child's teaching team is or is not following the IEP. You would most likely be asking for this type of meeting if you do not see progress within a quarter, term, or semester. You could also request this type of meeting if you notice that your child is regressing or sliding backwards.

Since these meetings can be particularly trying, it is very important to prepare yourself thoroughly and stick to the script. If you have a situation that might require a more personalized script or an _education consultation_, please _contact me_.

Parent: Thanks for meeting with me today. I have some concerns about how (Child's Name)'s IEP/504 Plan is being followed. Specifically *(explain your concerns here, use the list to help you):*

- not being pulled as required for therapies (speech, physical therapy, occupational therapy)

- not being pulled as required for core instruction (math, reading, writing)

- not being included as required for core content

- not being included as required for non-core content (social studies, science, specialists)

- special education teacher not assisting with core content instruction in the general education classroom as required (reading, writing, math)

- special education teacher not assisting with other content instruction in the general education setting as required(social studies, science)

- teacher(s) not tracking progress as required

- teacher not modifying workload in length or content at required

- assistive technology not being used as required (Braille typewriter, speech to text, iPad, communication device, etc.)

- preferential seating not being implemented

- behavioral modification systems not being implemented or not implemented correctly (ABA, reward system, etc.)

- lack of progress toward IEP/504 Plan goals; no work coming home

- testing accommodations/modifications not being followed (small group testing, read aloud, quiet setting, frequent breaks, etc.)

- lack of communication between school and home

- lack of leveled materials

- not differentiating, specifically for students who have both an IEP and are gifted/talented

Explain exactly where you are seeing the issue, what your concern is, and where you are getting your information from.

Parent: Could you please explain to me what is going on?

Teacher: *shares information related to your concerns. Some possible answers are:*

- lack of staffing beyond their control

- changes in schedules beyond their control

- special events/testing disrupting normal schedules

- student not responding to old behavior or work motivation techniques/systems

- student unable to complete work in the GT program, benefiting more from alternate instruction during that time

- teacher is pushing in, but student doesn't need direct help during all of that time

- students with conflicting personalities both need to be in the same areas of the room, your child has been moved to a non-preferred seat since that is better than sitting with the other child

- student is showing aptitude in subject, leading to longer/more challenging work in that area

- testing accommodations/modifications is only for certain kinds of tests, not regular classroom tests

- teacher is collecting work samples; will be returned at the end of the quarter/semester

- student is resistant to assistive technology/behavior modification programs/ academic work/teachers

Remember that teachers can be following the letter of the IEP exactly, but due to resistance from your child or issues beyond their control, there might be issues.

If the explanation is reasonable and understandable:

Parent: Thank you for explaining that to me. I understand that you are working against some road blocks. What can I do to help you?

Teacher: *explains if/how parent can help.*

Parent: Excellent. I will begin doing that immediately. If things are still going the same in a few weeks, I'd like to meet again or have a meeting with the whole IEP team to reassess what we are doing. Does that sound reasonable?

Teacher: Absolutely. I will be sure to keep you in the loop. Thank you for letting me know your concerns, and for understanding the situation.

If you do not think the explanation is reasonable or understandable:

Parent: While I appreciate what you just explained, I don't agree that it should be impacting my child's IEP/504 Plan. What can we do together to make sure that things change right away?

Teacher: *offers possible solutions. Understand that some solutions will require additional IEP/504 Plan meetings or approval from school administration*

Parent: I am willing to do what it takes to make this situation right and help my child. I will support your best efforts. However, I am going to be keeping a close eye on this and would like to follow up in two weeks.

At two week follow-up, ask for evidence that the plan has been implemented and for proof of progress. Know that two weeks is not enough time to work miracles or show huge growth. However, if things are still non-compliant with the IEP/504 Plan, request a meeting with the IEP/504 Plan team and school administration immediately.

Emails

There are many reasons to email the teacher. From routine inquiries to special concerns, it is important to format your emails in order to ensure maximum success.

Note: As s/he grows, especially in high school, your child should be taking the lead on sending these emails and having these conversations. Practicing these communication skills now will help to cement them for life.

The sample email templates in this section are just suggestions! Some emails can be used more generally or can be adapted for different situations. If you need help crafting a specific email, please contact me.

Crafting Subject Lines

Before you hit send on an email, make sure that the subject line is clear, concise, and logical.

In every subject line you should include:

- your child's name

- subject of the email

- any dates, chapter numbers, assignment titles (if applicable)

Examples:

- Susie Jones - Missing homework

- John Quinn - Low test grade on chapter 4 math

- Jane O'Brien - Make-up work for vacation 3/2-3/13

- Bobby Lee - Playground behavior with other 4th grade boys

- Kelsey Swart's mom - Volunteering in school next week

By including this information, the teacher is better able to determine the level of importance of each email. In the examples above, the teacher might respond to the emails about playground behavior issue and the low test grade first.

Keep in mind that teachers get dozens of emails daily from parents, other teachers, school administrators, and various organizations. Having a clear subject line will help your child's teacher address your concerns in a timely fashion.

Questions about Assignments
When you don't know if there are assignments

Dear (Teacher's Name),

I have missed checking (Child's Name)'s agenda book or the class website recently. Would you please let me know if there are any major projects, assignments, or tests coming up in the next few weeks? I definitely want to make sure (Child's Name) is prepared and has his/her work completed on time.

If you need any assistance with projects or classroom tasks, please let me know. I can help (explain how and when you can help).

Sincerely,

(Your Name)

When you don't understand the directions (homework)

Dear (Teacher's Name),

I see that (page number, problem, etc.) has been assigned as homework tonight. (Child's Name) is having trouble understanding and completing this work. I'm tried my best to help, but I also don't understand.

We will be leaving this problem blank. I apologize that this will be incomplete, but I don't want to explain this incorrectly and create more confusion. We would both appreciate it if you would review this concept tomorrow. If you have any links to videos or information for me, I would really like to learn how to do this type of work so I can help in the future.

Please let me know if you notice any concerns in class tomorrow.

Best,

(Your Name)

When you don't understand the directions (project)

Dear (Teacher's Name),

(Child's Name) is so excited about the project that you just assigned. I would love to help him/her at home, but I'm not quite sure what to do.

Could you send me a copy of the directions, rubric, and any other materials related to this project? I want to make sure I am following your instruction and not going off on a different path.

Thanks so much,

(Your Name)

Late or missing work, make ups

Dear (Teacher's Name),

Thank you for letting me know that (Child's Name) has late/missing work. Since this will likely affect his/her grade, would you be willing to provide the assignments for completion at home?

Either digital or hard copies of the work are fine. I will ensure that my child completes this work and returns it to you in a timely fashion.

I will be talking to him/her about this issue as well.

Best,

(Your Name)

Late or missing work, no make ups

Dear (Teacher's Name),

Thank you for letting me know about (Child's Name)'s missing/late work. I believe that my child needs to learn about personal responsibility.

I will be talking to (Child's Name) about this issue, and urging him/her to turn in the work. However, if it is not turned in by your deadline, please proceed accordingly. I understand that this could result in a lower grade for my child.

Thank you for letting me know about this issue.

(Your Name)

Emails about Grades

Child has an unusually low test grade

Dear (Teacher's Name),

I understand that (Child's Name) got a (grade) on the last test in (subject). I'm concerned as this is not like him/her.

Would you be able to shed some light on what you think might have happened? I want to make sure that I can talk to (Child's Name) about this, and correct it, before the next test.

Thanks so much,

(Your Name)

Child has multiple low test grades

Dear (Teacher's Name),

I have been noticing that (Child's Name) has been doing poorly in (subject). I'm very concerned about his/her recent test scores.

I very much want to address any concerns or issues before this gets out of control. Could you shed some light on what you are noticing in class? What are your recommendations? How can I support you at home?

Thanks so much,

(Your Name)

Low report card grade

Dear (Teacher's Name),

I saw (Child's Name)'s report card. The low grade(s) in (subject/subjects) are concerning to me. Could you please let me know what you are seeing in the classroom? I'd very much like to work together to get (Child's Name) back on the right track before the next report card.

I would like to meet in the next week or so to talk about this further. Let me know when you are available please.

Thanks so much,

(Your Name)

Low grade warning, response

Dear (Teacher's Name),

Thank you for letting me know that (Child's Name) is not doing well in (subject/subjects). Can you shed some light on what you are seeing in the classroom? What do you think is causing these low grades? How can we work together to correct these concerns and get (Child's Name) back on track?

Please let me know when you are available in the next two weeks. I would like to meet with you to talk about a plan to get (Child's Name) back on track.

Thanks so much,

(Your Name)

Behavior Concerns

Often, it is easiest and fastest to discuss behavior issues via email. If this happens, use these templates to help you respond to or inform the teacher about your concerns.

Remember to remain logical and as unemotional as possible. You need to get answers and facts. By using these email templates as your guide, it will help you to work with the teacher to find a solution.

If you are not satisfied with the response via email, you can always ask for an in-person meeting. For sample scripts to help you with these meetings, please turn to page 15. Having backup before or during contentious meetings can be very helpful. An education consultant can help you prepare or can advocate for your child on your behalf. To learn more about consulting services offered by MilKids Ed, contact me.

Behavior concerns, response

Dear (Teacher's Name),

Thank you for letting me know about the situation at school today. I am very concerned about this.

Could you provide some more information? When and where exactly did this happen? Did anything happen right before that might have caused this situation? How did you first know about this situation? If you didn't see it firsthand, could you direct me to a staff member who was there?

I understand that there will be consequences for (Child's Name) as a result of this. Could you please outline what exactly will happen? Do you think that there need to be consequences at home as well? If so, what do you think would be appropriate?

Please let me know if this continues to be a problem.

Sincerely,

(Your Name)

Behavior concerns, bullying

Dear (Teacher's Name),

I wanted to alert you to a situation with (Child's Name) at school (today, this week, recently).

(Explain situation as your child as presented it to you. Include names or initials of other students, locations, times, actions/reactions, etc.)

(Child's Name) has been deeply affected by this and is upset. As a parent, I want to make sure that s/he feels safe and welcome at school.

Can we work together to address this issue? Please let me know the next steps you plan to take and how I can support you.

Thanks so much for your help,

(Your Name)

Behavior concerns, disagreement

Dear (Teacher's Name),

Thank you for alerting me to my child's actions in school today. Would you please provide some more information? This behavior seems so out of character for (Child's Name).

I will be talking to him/her about this, but want to make sure I have enough information.

After I speak with him/her, I will email you again and let you know what we discussed. I'm truly having a hard time believing that s/he did this.

If possible, could we meet later this week to talk more about this?

Best,

(Your Name)

Behavior concerns, consequence disagreement

Dear (Teacher's Name),

Thank you so much for alerting me to my child's behavior in school today. While I appreciate your behavior and discipline policies, I have concerns about the consequences (Child's Name) received.

Would you be able to help me understand why these specific consequences were given to my child?

Is there an alternative consequence path available? If so, could we meet later this week to discuss this course of action?

Sincerely,

(Your Name)

Special Education

Before gathering the whole team for a Special Education meeting, try to hash out some details via email! Should you need help creating customized emails, <u>contact me</u> for information about <u>virtual education consulting services</u>.

Scheduling questions

Dear (Teacher's Name),

I have some questions about when and how often my child is being seen by (specialists, therapists, Special Education teachers/aides). Could you send me a quick overview of my child's schedule for a regular week?

I just want to be sure that s/he is being seen as often as the IEP/504 Plan requires. And you know how hard it is to get a straight answer out of kids!

I appreciate your help!

Sincerely,

(Your Name)

Content questions

Dear (Teacher's Name),

I was looking over (Child's Name)'s work recently and had some questions.

Could you shed some light on what s/he is doing in (subject/subjects)? The work I was seeing seemed to be (too easy/too hard/too much/not enough), and I wanted to double check with you that this fits within your standards and the IEP/504 Plan.

Please let me know right away if you have any concerns about (Child's Name).

Thank you,

(Your Name)

Lack of progress

Dear (Teacher's Name),

I wanted to let you know that we are very concerned that (Child's Name) is not making adequate progress toward (goal/goals) in (content area/social skill area/therapy area). After looking at the work s/he is bringing home, we are not seeing much improvement.

Could you let me know what you are seeing at school? If this is not your specific area, please feel free to forward this email with our concerns to the correct person.

I want to make sure that (Child's Name) is succeeding and moving forward. If there is anything that I can do at home to help support you at school, please let us know. I am more than happy to come in for a meeting or to explore tweaking the IEP/504 Plan.

Thank you so much for your hard work,

(Your Name)

Non-compliance

Dear (Teacher's Name),

Thank you so much for your hard work this year with (Child's Name). I wanted to contact you because we are concerned that the IEP/504 Plan is not being completely followed. We specifically have concerns about (content, schedule, therapy, pull out/push in, frequency, duration, work level, work length, test accommodations, lack of progress, etc.).

(Detail your concerns and provide specifics.)

I understand that you have a lot on your plate, and very much appreciate the time you're taking to look into this. I know we all want (Child's Name) to succeed to his/her highest potential.

Please send us an update on this situation as soon as possible. If we need to come in for a meeting, we would like to schedule that for as soon as possible as well.

Sincerely,

(Your Name)

Other Emails

There are many reasons to email the teacher. Use one of the following templates to communicate effectively and efficiently.

Make-up work, sick day

Dear (Teacher's Name)

As you know, (Child's Name) has been absent due to illness. Could you please provide the work she s/he missed during this time. I would like to make sure that s/he doesn't fall behind.

Please send the work (home with {name of a child in your neighborhood}/to the office where I will pick it up). If there are any videos or online resources for instruction, please let me know. We would love to watch a lesson or have instruction if any part of the work was recently introduced.

Thank you so much for your hard work,

(Your Name)

Make-up work, vacation or other absence

Dear (Teacher's Name),

(Child's Name) will be out of school from (date) to (date). If it is possible, could you please provide some work for him/her to do while s/he is away from the classroom?

We (will/will not) have access to the internet, so (online work will be completed/we would prefer paper work if possible).

Will my child be missing any tests or major projects during this time? If so, could we discuss a time after s/he returns to complete that work or take the tests? We are more than happy to work on projects at home, too.

Thank you for helping us. I know that this likely adds work to your plate. We very much appreciate your dedication to your students!

Best,

(Your Name)

Volunteering

Dear (Teacher's Name),

I would like to volunteer to help out in your classroom this year. I have volunteered in the past as (explain your previous volunteer roles, if any). I really enjoyed helping (Child's Name)'s teachers in past years.

I (am/am not) available during the school day.

What are the best ways that I could help you?

Sincerely,

(Your Name)

Phone Calls

Some phone calls from school may be upsetting, but they don't have to be. Use these ideas and prompts to stay calm and make the most of your phone call with the teacher.

Positive academic news

The teacher has called to tell you that your child:

- has good grades this quarter/semester

- has shown improvements recently

- has been accepted into the GT program

- is receiving special recognition for academic achievement

You respond:

- Wonderful! Thank you for sharing this good news with us!

- We're really proud of (Child's Name). We can tell s/he is working hard this year.

- Thank you so much for your hard work and dedication to teaching our child. S/he loves your class!

- How can we continue to support (Child's Name) together?

Negative academic news

The teacher has called to tell you that your child:

- has failed a test

- has an excessive amount of missing or late work

- has failed several tests

- has a low grade

- has a failing grade

- has not been putting forth effort

- has general academic concerns

- is in danger of repeating the class/grade

You respond:

- Thank you for letting me know about (academic concern). Can you explain a little bit more about what is going on?

- When did you first notice this issue? How long has this been going on?

- What approach have you been taking in the classroom?

- What can I do at home?

- Do you recommend a tutor? Is there a list at the school?

- Do you think that we should consider Special Education?

- Are there other things going on that might be causing (Child's Name) to fall behind? (Consider: life events, socializing with friends, time of year, time of day, absences, vacation, interest in subject, other students in class, seating arrangements, proximity to the board, etc.)

- Can my student (make up the work/raise his/her grade)?

- What is the school policy on repeating a class/grade?

- Are there programs at school that might help my child? (Consider: peer tutors, peer mentors, homework club, after school office hours, remedial courses, etc.)

- How can we work together to help (Child's Name) succeed?

- Can we meet in person to discuss this issue further?

Behavior, positive

The teacher calls to tell you that your child:

- showed empathy/sympathy to another child

- went above and beyond as a classroom helper

- was a good friend

- defended another student from bullying

- helped another student socially or academically

- helped a staff member

- is generally a great person

You respond:

- Thank you very much!

- We will be certain to pass on your kind words to (Child's Name) this evening.

- We are so happy that our child is showing strength of character.

- Please let us know how we can continue to guide our child in this direction.

Behavior, negative

The teacher calls to tell you that your child:

- has been bullying another student in an setting

- was physically aggressive/violent toward another student

- was physically aggressive/violent toward a staff member

- has been misusing classroom materials

- has violated the internet use policies

- has brought an unauthorized tech device to school

- has threatened staff or students verbally or in writing

- has used inappropriate language in any setting

- has been caught cheating

- has been caught stealing

- has been caught lying

- has been skipping class

You respond:

- Thank you for letting me know about this issue right away. I appreciate your prompt notification.

- Can you please explain the situation to me in greater detail?

- When and where did this happen?

- Who was involved?

- What led up to this situation?

- Who reported it/witnessed it? Is this person an adult or a child/student?

- What were the immediate steps taken when you learned of this situation?

- What are the school's policies for this type of behavior?

- (if something is broken) How much did (item) cost? How I can I replace (item)?

- (if another child is hurt) Please let the parents of the other child know how deeply sorry I am for my son/daughter's actions.

- (if you don't agree with the consequences) I would like to meet with you and the principal to discuss an alternative consequence for this action. I do not believe that what you are suggesting fits the action.

- Do there need to be additional consequences at home?

- (if your child is suspended) How do I go about getting the work for those days?

- (if your child has detention) When and where can I pick up my child?

- (if your child might face expulsion) I would like to have a meeting with you at the earliest possible time. Please let me know your availability

- We will be discussing this situation as a family. We will reiterate that this is not appropriate behavior and will talk about better ways to handle situations like these.

- Please let me know if this behavior continues.

Illness and injury
Your child has become ill or been injured at school. You say:

- What are the symptoms?

- When did they first occur?

- Where did they first occur?

- How did this happen? What events lead up to this injury?

- Have any steps been taken? (EpiPen, calling 911, giving medication, bandaging a wound, etc.)

- Is there need for further treatment?

- Where can I pick up my child?

- Is this possibly contagious?

- Does the school have a policy about returning following illness? (such as the 24-hour rule for vomiting and fevers)

- Thank you for letting me know about this and for caring for my child. I truly appreciate your dedication.

Understanding the School Hierarchy

Different people in schools handle different things. An issue in the classroom shouldn't immediately involve the principal. Before you send that email or pick up the phone, consult this list.

Teachers

- Academic concerns

    - grades

    - tests

    - projects

    - assignments

    - homework

    - classwork

    - curriculum content

    - subject(s) taught

- Classroom set-up

    - seating assignments

    - decor

    - displayed work

- IEP/504 Plan (involve the general and Special Education teachers)

    - modifications

    - accommodations

    - noncompliance (first communication, follow up meeting)

- Behavior

    - bullying

- disruptive behavior

- off-task

- first offenses: stealing, lying, cheating

- Volunteering in the classroom

- field trips

Special Education Teachers

- IEP

- 504 Plan

- Academics related to the IEP/504 Plan

- Schedule of specialists, therapists

- Changes to education plans

Administration

The principal and vice principal should be the last resort contacts. It's not that they don't want to know about your concerns. It's that things related to the classroom and your child should be handled with the classroom teacher first. Administrators should only be called in for classroom concerns if the teacher refuses to work with you or if no progress has been made after a reasonable period of time.

If you do contact the administration before the teacher for a classroom-specific concern, the teacher might feel like you do not respect her professionally or personally. Before you contact administration, please do your very best to resolve any issues or concerns with the classroom teacher or special education teacher first. If you need help, an education consultant can assist you with this process. Contact me to learn more about personalized education consulting services.

- Serious behaviors

- physical violence

- threats to well-being of self or others

- weapons

- repeat offenders: stealing, lying, cheating
- bullying

- Academics: when the teacher is not working with you or no progress has been made after a reasonable period of time

- Teacher negligence or misconduct

Office Staff

- Records: report cards, permanent records, test results

- Enrolling/disenrolling

- Attendance/absences

- General communications about the school

- Directing further communication to other staff

Tips for Effective Communication

Whether you are talking face-to-face, via email, or over the phone, it is important to remember a few key things.

- Tone matters. Make sure that you avoid sarcasm in text or on the phone. It is hard to read and could be taken the wrong way. It could set a negative tone for any future communication.

- Ask questions. Before you make a final decision or judgement call, it's important to have all the details. You won't know unless you ask!

- Take notes. Get the details in writing, especially about education plans or things that the teacher is going to do.

- Double check and clarify everything. It never hurts to make sure you have the details right the first time. Show the teacher your notes and ask if this is also his/her understanding of your discussion for future plans.

- Follow up. Give it a few days post-meeting, then send an email to check on progress from the meeting. Send another email in a week or so. Then reconfirm the plan and progress at your next meeting.

- Loop the teacher in on anything related to this issue. If it impacts your child, the teacher should know. If not, things might not proceed as smoothly otherwise.

- Be respectful of the teacher's time. Emailing, calling, or requesting meetings outside of the working or school day should be avoided as much as possible. If you must email or call before or after school hours, allow your child's teacher a full working day or twenty-four hours to respond.

- When requesting that your child receive additional attention through specialized lessons, it is considerate to offer to finance materials above and beyond the school-provided items. Many teachers are happy to provide students enrichment or reteaching materials out of their own salaries, but parents who offer to help with these items financially often reap extra benefits and a better parent-teacher relationship

Education Terms to Know

Use these terms to help you navigate the K-12 education world. By reviewing this glossary, you will be better able to understand the teacher and improve communication during your meetings or conversations. Words have been grouped by topic or with other related words. Should you have questions about terminology that your teacher is using, please contact me.

Education Consultant: An individual with experience in K-12 schools, usually with classroom teaching credentials and advanced degrees. This person provides qualified advice to your family privately to better prepare you to meet the challenges at schools. Education consultants can review academic records, interpret assessment results, provide advice for at-home learning, help to set up a homeschool curriculum, problem solve homework battles, and work with you to communicate with your child's school in order to get results. Consultants are unable to offer legal advice.

Education Advocate: An individual with education law, teaching, and/or Special Education experience, usually with advanced degrees in one or more of these fields. Education advocates work with families before, during, and after meetings with schools, particularly special education meetings. Advocates work on behalf of their clients to ensure the best possible outcome for the student. As a third party with experience with or in a school system, advocates are uniquely qualified to see both sides of the table and help to broker compromises that benefit the student. Advocates may have experience in education law, but may or may not be lawyers. Advocates without law degrees provide legal advice, which families follow at their own discretion and responsibility. Lawyers should be consulted with specific concerns.

Education Lawyer: A lawyer who specializes in education law. Education lawyers are usually a last step during contentious education situations, as their services may be costly. Education lawyers are the only individuals qualified to give firm legal advice to clients, and should be consulted with concerns about advice from education consultants and advocates.

Meet the Teacher: Typically, this is a day held the week before school resumes. Parents and their children go to their new classrooms, meet the teacher(s), and acclimate themselves for the first day of school. This is a chance to put a face with a name, locate your child's desk, and help ease nervous energy. For scripts to use on Meet the Teacher day, please see page 10.

Parent-Teacher Conference: This can be any face-to-face meeting between parents and a teacher or teachers. Often, parent-teacher conference is a name given to a specific scheduled meeting time held after the first grading period of the year. Parents can schedule other conferences throughout the year, based on need and availability.

Special Education: a program that provides qualified students with additional or modified instruction based on their academic and/or related physical, social, emotional, behavioral, and/or language needs. Students receiving special education services may have either an IEP or a 504 Plan.

Special Education Referral: Being notified of a referral to Special Education means that your child has been receiving interventions in the classroom, and that those interventions are not working for him/her (see: Response to Intervention, pg 55). There should be extensive documentation of the attempted interventions, assessment results, and notes from the teacher(s).

At this point, you have the right to decline Special Education by refusing to allow testing. You also have the right to request Special Education testing for your child.

IEP: Individual Education Plan. An education plan created for an individual student based on diagnosis or assessment data as related to one of thirteen disability categories. IEPs are federal legal documents and must be followed as written by all staff working with that child. IEPs end when the child has made adequate progress and is working at grade level or they graduate from high school or reach the end of their public school's special education program, usually at age 21 or 22.

An IEP changes the content and delivery of instruction. Subjects may be presented at a lower level, in a separate setting, or by the special education teacher in the general education classroom. Often support services, like speech therapy, occupational therapy, or physical therapy, are included in IEPs.

504 Plan: Similar to an IEP, but is valid throughout life. The content of the curriculum is not changed and the student is expected to work on grade level. The environment is able to be changed. Examples would include:

- ramps for wheelchairs

- wider aisles in the classroom to improve navigation

- Braille machines or books

- speech to text software, computer access, communication devices

- additional testing time, small group testing, quiet setting for tests

- large print books, audio books

Students with 504 Plans may also receive support services like speech, occupational, physical, or behavioral therapies.

Modification: A modification is any change to the content of the curriculum or learning materials. This means similar topics presented at a lower or higher reading level, shortened assignments, and alternative instruction. Modifications are standard for IEPs. Many teachers will modify work to meet your child's needs without an IEP. However, for extensive modifications or changes that are significantly below your child's current grade level/age, you should seek a referral to Special Education services. For specifics about possible modifications, <u>schedule a consult with me</u>.

Accommodation: An accommodation is a change to the physical environment or delivery of the curriculum. The content and level of the curriculum remains the same. The only changes would help your child access the materials. There are many standard accommodations in everyday life: wheelchair ramps, Braille signs, ASL interpreters at events. There are also many classroom accommodations available to your child: large print or audio books, speech-to-text word processing, preferential seating, extended testing or assignment time. For more information about how MilKids Ed can help your child receive accommodations, <u>email me</u>.

Special Education Team: The team of teachers, specialists/therapists, and administrators who manage your child's IEP or 504 Plan. These professionals are responsible for following the IEP or 504 Plan and working with your child to meet annual goals.

Annual Review: IEPs and 504 Plans are required to be reviewed, discussed, and revised at least once every year. Other reviews may be scheduled at any time to discuss concerns or potential changes to the document.

Triennial Review: Every three years, your child's IEP or 504 Plan will be completely reviewed to determine if your child is still eligible. Your child will be retested in the previously identified eligible categories, as well as assessing any new areas of concern. Based on the results of these new tests, your child will either continue with the IEP or 504 Plan or exit the system to the general education classroom. Students who are no longer eligible under IEP rules may still be able to receive services under 504 Plan categories.

Response to Intervention (RtI): This is a program in place in many schools throughout the US. Students in this program are given specialized academic interventions using research-based methods. Students may be assisted in the classroom, may be removed from the classroom to work with a different teacher, or may receive a combination of these methods. Meticulous records are kept, along with work samples, to show any progress a student might make. Students who do not make progress with one method may continue in the program using different instruction techniques and tools until they do make progress. Students who continue to show no progress may be referred for special education services.

Gifted and Talented (GT): This is a type of program that goes by many names at many schools. Generally, GT programs are for students who have been found eligible through testing, referrals, or observations. Students have demonstrated high intelligence or exceptional skill in an academic area. GT programs are supposed to be designed to facilitate deeper exploration of grade level content, inspire higher level thinking, and improve logical education. Each GT program is different; however, none of them should be exclusively workbook-based.

Assessments: Assessments are formal, standardized tests of all kinds. All students will be assessed, or tested, throughout their academic careers.

All students, unless exempted by an IEP, will take state or national standardized tests. This would be tests similar to the PARCC, IOWA tests, SAT, and ACT. All students will also take benchmarking tests (example: STAR) to see where they are at in math and language arts at points throughout the year.

Scores from these tests will be compared to national norms, or averages, to determine where your is on a scale. Each tests has a different standard score scale, however they usually have a percentile rank. A rank of 50 equals average. However, most schools want scores to be above average. Scores significantly above average (85-90+) are considered excellent. Scores significantly below average (less than 45-40) are considered at risk.

All students will also take classroom or grade level tests based directly on content they have recently learned. These tests are based directly on the content and connected learning standards. They may be designed by a publishing company (example: McGraw-Hill) or created by the classroom or grade level teachers.

Special Education Assessments: In Special Education, assessments are used to diagnose and identify disabilities or learning differences. Specially trained assessors or evaluators are used to ensure that the assessments are given as directed, scored correctly, and interpreted with validity. Common Special Education assessments target IQ, aptitude vs. achievement (what a student can do vs. what they actually do), speech, social abilities, physical abilities (fine and gross motor skills), life skills, behaviors, attentiveness, and more. If there is a concern, there is usually a standardized assessment for it.

In Special Education, assessments are used to determine eligibility. Assessors and teachers are looking for scores that show a wide discrepancy, such as a child with a very high IQ performing several grade levels lower than expected.

Behavior: While the term includes positive and negative actions, parents who are called in to discuss behavior concerns are typically going to be working through negative behaviors. Negative behaviors could range from very mild (white lies) to moderate (stealing personal property like pencils; cheating) to very serious (bullying; stealing expensive items. threatening violence).

Classroom teachers will often work with parents for behavior concerns on the mild to moderate end of the spectrum. Students with more pressing to serious situations will likely be working with the teacher and/or the administration team of principal or vice principal.

Enrichment: Students who are demonstrating abilities above and beyond grade level, or students who finish work early, are often offered additional opportunities to learn. These can involve projects, extra assignments, targeted learning techniques, or the Gifted and Talented programs.

Many teachers today have enrichment opportunities built into their classrooms. Through fast-finisher folders, leveled groupings, and differentiated assignments, most students in schools are receiving enriched activities throughout their academic careers.

Leveled Groups/Small Groups: Students do not all work at the same level, and it is unfair to ask them to learn at the same speed. To accommodate students across the spectrum, teachers often strategically group students together to provide a better learning experience for everyone. Different groups will be working at different levels: reteaching, on grade level, or advanced. Groups may stay the same across subjects or when introducing new content, however most groups will have variations in membership.

Teachers work hard to keep students feeling positive by naming groups with neutral terms and not broadcasting which group is "high" or "low."

Individual Instruction/1:1 Instruction: Often students with IEPs or other academic concerns need targeted attention. Teachers will work with these students separately to improve specific skills, help with a project, or work through classroom situations.

Push-in: When a Special Education teacher or paraprofessional (aide) enters your child's general education classroom to specifically work with one or more students using specialized teaching materials or learning strategies.

Pull-out: Students will leave the general education setting to work with a Special Education teacher or paraprofessional in a different location. Students who receive pull-out services generally work with different standards, materials, or techniques than their classroom peers. Pulling students out of the classroom can help them to focus and not call attention to the discrepancies in level or ability.

Support Services: These include speech and language therapy, occupational therapy, physical therapy, behavior modification (ABA), social skills, and/or mental health. Students receiving support in these areas might have additional support in the classroom through push-in teaching, or may be pulled-out to a separate setting. Students identified as receiving Special Education services via an IEP or 504 Plan may receive these services. Any child is able to receive additional mental health support.

Rubric: A method of grading that divides an assignment into components. Each component is described and rated based on level of completion. Students receive a rating on each part of the project, and the points are totaled for the final grade.

Rating Scale: Students are given a numeric score based on their performance on a given task. Generally, a higher rating means a better performance on the task.

Cumulative Grade: A final grade that incorporates all grades received in a designated period of time. All grades are added together, then divided by the total number of graded assignments during that period to calculate the final score.

Students who did poorly on one or more major assignments, or who started with very poor scores before improving, might receive lower scores that do not accurately reflect their knowledge in an area.

Standards Based Grading: Students are graded or rated based on their mastery of given standards or skills at their grade level. This method of grading takes into account student growth, effort, and final achievement. Students are not penalized for low scores during the introduction of new skills or content; only their final outcomes are assessed.

Twenty-four Hour Rule: When students have a fever (over 100.4F or school specified temperature), are vomiting, or have diarrhea, they should stay home until the condition has been controlled without medication for 12-24 hours. This is for the safety of other students and school staff, as well as for the well-being of your child. A child who is sick will not be able to fully concentrate or absorb information. Additionally, their body will be spending valuable energy fighting through the school day instead of healing. This rule should also be observed with other contagious illness, like pink eye, influenza, and severe colds.

Family Vacation: This is any lengthy scheduled absence from school. For trips that will remove the child from the classroom for 1-2 days, it is usually not necessary to request make-up work in advance. For longer trips or absences, request work to complete while your child is away from school. If you are requesting work, be mindful that your child should complete the work for submission when s/he returns to school.

Make-up Work: This is work that your child will be required to complete due to absence from school. This work will come home with your child following an absence, be delivered to your home by a friend or neighbor, or can be requested in advance by you. Work requested in advance may only be supplemental, since actual graded assignments in the classroom may vary from what your child has received. After receiving make-up work, please ensure that your child completes this work as quickly as possible.

Consequences: When dealing with negative behaviors, there are often consequences involved. These should almost always relate to the specific behavior and should not include arbitrary menial labor. An exception to this might be if a child defaces property and then must clean it.

Consequences should not prevent the student from eating lunch or staying hydrated. Consequences should also not totally remove recess or other movement breaks.

For more serious consequences, a loss of privileges, additional homework or explanatory writing project, detention, suspension, or expulsion might be considered.

When discussing consequences, it is best to become familiar with the school's discipline policy and code of conduct.

Parent Records and Worksheets

As you attend meetings, make phone calls, and write emails, it is important to keep a record of what happens.

How to keep records

Making and keeping records, especially of communication, takes practice and diligence.

The first step is to have a recording sheet of every point of contact that you make. For this, use the Communication Log on <u>page 63</u>. Maintain separate logs for each of your children. Best practice would be to have binders or folders dedicated to each child in your house to keep communication records, meeting worksheets, and important school documents, like report cards of IEPs.

Whenever you call, email, or meet with a teacher, make note of:

- the child the meeting is about

- the date and time

- the method of communication

- the location of the communication, if meeting in person

- other people included in the email, call, or meeting

- purpose of the meeting

- the script or template that you used

In your binder, keep the hard copies of the worksheet that you used, any documents, and your notes about the meeting, email, or call. You could even go so far as to print out the emails. Another option would be to file school-related emails in your inbox by school year or area of concern (see below).

As you are filing your records, keep them in chronological order. To get very neat, separate your records by type:

- behavior

- IEP/504 Plan

- Gifted and Talented

- other academics

- volunteering, field trips, social

- other

Having orderly, complete files that are easy to access and navigate will help you throughout your child's academic career. It will be very easy to track who you have communicated with, when, and about what. You will also have a paper trail of education plans, specific conversations, and plans you have made with the teacher. Having good records can help everyone to stay on track and maintain their responsibilities.

Should there be disputes down the line, complete records can help you and your <u>education consultant</u> to work through a situation.

School Communication Log for _____

Date	Method of Communication	Reason	Teacher	Script page #
	email phone meeting			
	email phone meeting			
	email phone meeting			
	email phone meeting			
	email phone meeting			
	email phone meeting			
	email phone meeting			
	email phone meeting			
	email phone meeting			
	email phone meeting			
	email phone meeting			
	email phone meeting			
	email phone meeting			
	email phone meeting			
	email phone meeting			
	email phone meeting			
	email phone meeting			
	email phone meeting			
	email phone meeting			
	email phone meeting			
	email phone meeting			
	email phone meeting			
	email phone meeting			
	email phone meeting			
	email phone meeting			
	email phone meeting			
	email phone meeting			

Phone Call Record Sheet

Date:_____   **Time:**_____

Child:_____

Teacher:_____

Script page number/title:_____

Reason for call:

_____

_____

_____

_____

_____

_____

_____

My questions:

_____

_____

_____

_____

_____

_____

Teacher next steps:

_____

_____

_____

My next steps:

_____

_____

_____

Follow up:

Email ☐ date sent:_____ reply received:_____

Phone call ☐ date received:_____

Meeting ☐ date scheduled:_____ location:_____

Email Notes

Date:_____ **Time:**_____

Child:_____

Teacher:_____

Email template page number/title:

_____

Reason for email:

_____
_____
_____
_____
_____

My immediate reaction:

_____
_____
_____
_____
_____
_____
_____
_____

Reply sent: Yes   No

Date:_____

Follow up:

Email ☐ date sent:_____ reply received:_____

Phone call ☐ date received:_____

Meeting ☐ date scheduled:_____ location:_____

Parent-Teacher Conference Worksheets

When you are getting ready for and attending a parent-teacher or parent-administrator meeting it is important to be prepared.

Following a script can help to keep meetings on track and work towards a positive resolution. However, a script is only as good as the preparation work behind it.

When you or your child's teacher requests a meeting, it is time for you to start getting ready.

First, located and print or copy any written communications, like emails. Include with these your completed copies of any email notes (page 64). At the same time, make copies of your phone call record sheets (page 63) and a copy of your master communication log (page 62).

Keep all of your communication records in chronological order.

Next, find and copy any other documents that relate to your meeting. It is important to make copies so that you can make notes while you plan. In addition, bringing courtesy copies of these documents to meetings is helpful to teachers and school staff. Examples of documents can include IEPs, 504 Plans, report cards, progress reports, work samples, test results, and student work samples.

Once all of your documents are assembled, it's time to really plan out your meeting.

Decide what you want the ideal outcome to be. What do you want to happen as a result of this meeting? Write it down on your parent-teacher conference planning worksheet (page 66). Remember that you may not get your perfect outcome. It can be helpful to write down other acceptable options as well.

As you are planning, flip through the parent-teacher conference sample scripts (starting on page 8). to find the one that best suits your needs. Print it out and make notes on it. Insert exactly the points that you need to bring up on the script itself. When it is time for your meeting, bring the script in with you.

At the meeting, bring in all of your documents, communication records, the parent-teacher conference planning worksheet, the script with your notes, and a copy of the parent-teacher conference notes worksheet (page 68).

It can help to work through meeting planning with an education consultant. To get help with your meeting, email me.

Parent-Teacher Conference Planning Worksheet

Date of meeting:_____

Time of meeting:_____

Location of meeting:_____

Child:_____

Teachers/school personnel scheduled to attend:

_____

_____

_____

Reason for meeting:

_____

_____

_____

_____

_____

My immediate reaction to situation:

_____

_____

_____

_____

_____

_____

Possible solutions:

_____

_____

_____

_____

_____

_____

What my child needs from the teacher/school/administrators:

_____
_____
_____
_____
_____

What I need from the teacher/school/administrators:

_____
_____
_____
_____
_____

What the teacher/school/administrators need from me:

_____
_____
_____
_____
_____

Documents to bring:

- ☐ IEP
- ☐ 504 Plan
- ☐ Emails
- ☐ Phone logs
- ☐ Work samples
- ☐ Report cards
- ☐ Tests/test analysis
- ☐ Other: _____

_____

Parent-Teacher Conference Notes

Date of meeting:_____

Time of meeting:_____

Location of meeting:_____

Child:_____

Teachers/school personnel scheduled to attend:

_____

_____

_____

Reason for meeting:

_____

_____

_____

_____

_____

Documents to bring:

☐ IEP

☐ 504 Plan

☐ Emails

☐ Phone logs

☐ Work samples

☐ Report cards

☐ Tests/test analysis

☐ Other: _____

_____

_____

Things to talk about:

1. _____

2. _____

3. _____

4. _____

5. _____

6. _____

Notes:

_____

_____

_____

_____

_____

_____

_____

_____

_____

_____

_____

_____

_____

_____

_____

_____

_____

Final resolution:

_____

_____

_____

_____

_____

_____

After this meeting, I will:

_____

_____

_____

_____

_____

After this meeting, the teacher will:

_____

_____

_____

_____

_____

After this meeting, school administrators will:

_____

_____

_____

_____

_____

Follow up:

Email ☐ date sent:_____ reply received:_____

Phone call ☐ date received:_____

Meeting ☐ date scheduled:_____ location:_____

After this meeting, I feel:

satisfied   neutral   dissatisfied

Notes on progress:

_____

_____

_____

_____

_____

About the Author

Meg Flanagan has been in education since 2009. After earning her Master's degree in Special Education from Bridgewater State University, Meg launched a private tutoring company focusing on military children. Since then, she has taught in public, private, and home schools.

Meg is the owner of MilKids Ed, a blog and consulting resource for military families. MilKids Ed offers timely articles and information about K-12 education for military children. Meg also is available to help your family navigate the K-12 journey.

For more information, please email Meg at milkidsed@@gmail.com. MilKids is also on Facebook, Instagram, Twitter, and Pinterest.

Made in the USA
Coppell, TX
22 December 2020